Jamali-Kamali

Jamali-Kamali

A Tale of Passion in Mughal India

Karen Chase

Introduction by
Milo Beach

*Mapin*Lit
AN IMPRINT OF
MAPIN PUBLISHING

First published in India in 2011 by
Mapin Publishing Pvt. Ltd
502 Paritosh, Near Darpana Academy,
Usmanpura Riverside, Ahmedabad 380013
T: 91 79 4022 8228 • F: 91 79 4022 8201
E: mapin@mapinpub.com
www.mapinpub.com

Simultaneously published in the
United States of America in 2010 by
Grantha Corporation
77 Daniele Drive, Hidden Meadows
Ocean Township, NJ 07712
E: mapin@mapinpub.com

Distributors
North America:
Antique Collectors' Club
T: 1 800 252 5231 • E: info@antiquecc.com
www.antiquecollectorsclub.com

Southeast Asia:
Paragon Asia Co. Ltd
T: 66 2877 7755 • F: 2468 9636
E: info@paragonasia.com

Australia & New Zealand
Peribo Pty Ltd
T: 61 2 9457 0011
E: michael.coffey@peribo.com.au

Distributed in the rest of the world by
Mapin Publishing Pvt. Ltd

ISBN: 978-81-89995-12-6 (Mapin)
ISBN: 978-1-935677-05-5 (Grantha)
LCCN: 2010934774

Editor: Vinutha Mallya / Mapin Editorial
Design: Revanta Sarabhai / Mapin Design Studio

Printed in India

Contents

For my sons
David and Matthew

Acknowledgements

Jamali–Kamali was set in motion while I was in Delhi enjoying a writing residency at the Sanskriti Pratishthan, founded by O.P. Jain. His vision and support resulted in the archeological restoration of the Jamali–Kamali Mosque and Tomb. Heartfelt thanks to O.P. Jain.

Jaya Sankrityayana Parhawk, my dear and encouraging friend who managed the residency program, put me in touch with a Persian scholar from York, England, so that my flood of questions could receive expert answers. Great gratitude to Jaya.

Bruce Wannell is that expert. Via email, he provided a rich, steady stream of cultural and historical information. He raised challenging questions. For this poem, Bruce travelled to the tomb and translated Jamali's verses which ring the ceiling. All the above added inspiration so no amount of thanks is enough for Bruce.

Didi Goldenhar and Jeffrey Harrison, best of poets and best of friends, each read several drafts of the poem and offered invaluable criticism. Lifelong thanks to you both.

After the poet Rennie McQuillkin read the manuscript, he sent it to his old school friend, the Mughal scholar Milo Beach, who sent it the publisher Bipin Shah. To these three men, much gratitude for taking the poem from my desk out to the world. And to my friend Mary Bisbee-Beek, many thanks to a unique publicist.

To Jonathan Matson, my literary agent, who stands by me always to follow art's circuitous route no matter what, great thanks.

To Willard Spiegelman, Scott Laugenour and Mark Woodward, my enormous thanks to each of you. Without such friendships, I suspect I would not have felt so linked to Jamali and Kamali.

And to Paul, my first reader always, thanks Love.

Jamali-Kamali: The Beauty of a Dervish Cell

Milo Beach

The Mosque and Tomb of Jamali–Kamali is not a large compound. Only a short distance south of one of the most heavily visited tourist sites in Delhi, the Qutb Minar, it remains isolated and quiet. Divided highways and compacted housing have recently invaded the area, but these have been kept well away, and the land outside the low enclosure walls, now a public park, is wooded. A sense of discovery, therefore, still accompanies visits. When I first explored the area forty years ago, the region was not only isolated, it was remote. Then, approaching the enclosure of the mosque across desolate fields—the latrines of nearby villagers and local wildlife—was an adventure. But it was the tiny tomb in its own walled courtyard to the north that really took one's breath away. Decorated on the outside with fragments of the original coloured tile work, the inside held the finest, most perfect incised and painted plaster of any monument in India. I had not dared go back since seeing it again in 1979, because graffiti flourishes so abundantly in unprotected monuments. Those fears, however, were groundless. The complex has recently been well restored, and now Karen Chase's poem brings it even further to life.

The tomb is an extremely simple structure architecturally, providing tangible testament to Jamali's personal

Mosque of Jamali–Kamali, c. 1528

humility. Single-storey, the exterior is decorated with small, decorative arched recesses, as well as the remaining tiles. A doorway facing the mosque leads into a modest square room—the most basic of living spaces. Its visual impact, however, is sumptuous.

The walls consist of plaster carved with intricately interlaced arabesques, and above arched windows in the center of each side a broad octagonal configuration provides transition to a narrow sixteen-sided cornice. Decorated with a carved band of poetry, this in turn supports a flat, circular ceiling richly decorated with sunbursts and floral forms in carved plaster, coloured (like the walls) in red and blue. The verses are those of Jamali, as is the calligraphy's design[1]—a confirmation of his identity with the structure. Undomed and architecturally unpretentious, it is the beauty of the ornament—as well as the intimate size of the space—that distinguishes the building.

Tomb of Jamali–Kamali, c. 1528

The tomb and the adjacent mosque are among the earliest buildings datable to the period of the Mughal emperors, who arrived in India in 1526 and later built much bigger monuments well to the north of these fields. This area of Delhi had housed the capital of a Rajput (Hindu) dynasty, whose defeat by the Muslim Qutbuddin Aibak in 1193 inaugurated a period when this and adjoining regions were ruled by Muslim Sultans. Mosques and tombs, and the remains of palaces, caravanserais (rest stops for travellers) and bazaars are spread across a landscape increasingly devastated by modern development. Here the saintly Khwaja Qutb-ud-din Bakhtiyar Kaki (known as Qutb Sahib) died in 1236. A disciple of the Sufi Sheikh Mu'in-ud-din Chishti, whose shrine (*dargah*) at Ajmer is India's holiest Muslim site, Qutb Sahib himself was highly venerated, and his dargah too became a place of great sanctity. The famed Moroccan traveller Ibn Battuta

Blue and white tiles under exterior eaves of the tomb

visited the tomb soon after his arrival in Delhi in 1334, noting that, "The blessed power of this tomb is manifest and it enjoys great veneration."[2] It was within the aura of Qutb Sahib that Sheikh Jamali—among many others—chose to live, and where he arranged to be buried.

Al-Badaoni, historian to the Mughal Emperor Akbar (r. 1556–1605), wrote in the late-sixteenth century that Sheikh Jamali "was one of the greatest among the Ulama Shaikhs of his time."[3] Born near Delhi about 1483, Jamali was famously peripatetic, his visits extending from Sri Lanka to southern Spain.[4] Badaoni further reports that he "was a man who travelled much, and had been honoured with the fellowship of our master the saintly Jami"[5] (among Iran's greatest Sufi poets). Jamali, a musician as well as a poet, also spent time in Herat at the court of the Timurid dynasty Sultan Husain Mirza

Upper walls and ceiling of the tomb's interior

(r. 1469–1506), patron of Behzad—the most famous of all Persian painters—and a great connoisseur of the arts. There he also befriended Mir Ali Shir Nava'i, another of that era's illustrious poets, and there too he would have seen the finest illustrations and encountered the greatest poems and musicians then known in the Islamic world. This was a period held up by the later Mughal emperors as a model; they constantly sought to emulate its artistic richness. It must therefore be these experiences, rather than chance, which makes Sheikh Jamali's tomb so beautifully decorated a monument. But while, in keeping with the customs of the time, the general vocabulary of the ornament is one widely dispersed throughout the wider Persian world, a distinctive exception is the band of blue and white tiles found under the eaves of the exterior. While the other building materials, the stones of the building and the pigments used for colours,

The tombstones of Jamali and Kamali

were almost certain of local origin, these tiles are not. In a ceramic technique then seemingly unknown in India proper, these may have been imported, representing one of Jamali's specific cosmopolitan contacts.

Jamali was a favourite of Sultan Sikandar Lodi (r. 1489–1517), whose dynasty preceded that of the Mughals in north India. According to Badaoni, "Among the poets of the time of Sikandar was the aforementioned Shaikh Jamali… of Dihli, to whom Sultan Sikandar was in the habit of submitting verses which he had written, for his opinion"[6]—certainly an uncommon accolade. It also shows, however, an informality among rulers and intelligentsia greater than that usual under the burgeoning imperiality of the Mughals. Sikandar Lodi's tomb lies in what is known today as the Lodi Gardens, an area now surrounded by the bungalows of New Delhi, the city constructed after

Tomb of Sultan Sikandar Lodi, c. 1517–18

1911 when the British decided to shift their capital from Calcutta. Nearby is a mosque constructed by Sikandar in 1494 and also adorned with superb decorations of incised plaster. Despite its Mughal date, the vocabulary of ornament found in Sheikh Jamali's tomb, and the level of its craftsmanship, are indistinguishable in quality from that found in Sikandar's monuments. (Only later—under the emperor Akbar—does Mughal architecture become truly innovative in structure and decorative motifs.) Those of sufficient status and favour at court must therefore have been able on occasion to draw upon imperial artists and craftsmen, although in this case the builders may also have been seeking work to fill their time as the new Mughal dynasty was assembling its power and defining its initial projects. Nonetheless, given his knowledge, sophistication, and interests, Jamali would almost certainly have directed the building's planning and construction.

Tomb of Balban, c. 1280. *See reference in pp 31 and 34*

Sheikh Jamali is not associated only with poetry and literati interests. The first Mughal Emperor Babur (r. 1526–1530) mentions Jamali in his memoirs under the entry for February 24, 1527, stating that "Shaykh Jamali was sent to assemble as many yeoman from... Delhi as he could, strike and plunder the villages of Mewat [a region south of the city], and do everything he could to harass the enemy from that direction."[7] On another occasion he was dispatched as an imperial emissary, to deliver a decree of safe conduct.[8] This military usefulness continued under Babur's son Humayun (r. 1530–1540; 1555–1556), for it was on a Mughal campaign in Gujarat that Jamali died in 1536 C.E. (H. 942). Humayun had "visited his [Jamali's] dervish-cell several times,"[9] a sign of the greatest respect for Jamali's religious persona, and the Sheikh's *Siyar al'arifin*, which contains biographies of various saints of the Chishti order, is dedicated to that emperor. Jamali was a man of remarkable range and abilities—and contacts.

Tomb of Jamali–Kamali—the interior chamber

Just as pleasure gardens constructed and enjoyed by the Mughals in life often became the location for their tombs after death, so Sheikh Jamali's "dervish-cell," was almost certainly on the site—and was probably the buildingthat housed his tomb. The term "cell," after all, suggests a simple single room, although if Jamali was known as a dervish, a Muslim ascetic, this would have reflected his physical needs more than the richness of his mental life.

The exact details—and dates—of the construction of both mosque and tomb are disputed by scholars, but no-one questions the architectural importance of the mosque, however modest Jamali's house may have been. While drawing on recognized Lodi dynasty prototypes, it is a forerunner of the superb mosque in what is now known as the Purana Qila (Old Fort), a building midway between the Jamali–Kamali site and the Red Fort, constructed in the 1640s by the Mughal Emperor Shah Jahan and visited by every tourist to Delhi. The great Purana Qila was built as the centre of a new capital alternately by the Mughal Emperor Humayun and his nemesis, an Afghan interloper who forced him into temporary exile. Jamali lived in times of transition, but even when the Mughal dynasty was an important new power within India, the mosque and tomb associated with Sheikh Jamali quietly served to link the Mughals with the considerable achievements of the earlier Lodis.

Carr Stephen, in his 1876 study of Delhi's architecture, wrote that Jamali built the mosque and a room to serve as living quarters in 1528 C.E. (H. 935). He noted that the tomb contained two graves, the other "supposed to be that of one Kamali, a brother of Jamali, but for this statement I have been unable to find any authority. The two graves are... without any ornamentation or inscription".[10] Later scholars repeat this date with variations. Giles Tillotson, for example, places construction between 1528 and 1536,[11] while the identification of Kamali as a brother of Sheikh Jamali is often repeated by others, sometimes as speculation and sometimes as fact (but never with corroborating evidence, since there is none). Karen Chase notes that local oral tradition believes the so-called Kamali to have been a male companion or lover, in keeping with accepted Sufi imagery and the character of Jamali's verses. This could easily be the remnants of earlier bazaar gossip, and her poem may authentically reflect what was in the minds of many of Jamali's contemporaries. Yet if we still have no unquestioned proof of the identity of this second burial, that it was a man is certain. Male tombstones were distinguished by the inclusion on the stone slab of a symbolic pen box (which we see on both cenotaphs here), while that of a woman customarily held the more passive shape of a writing tablet—that on which the pen inscribed.

Throughout the Delhi region, Sultanate and Mughal monuments abound; sometimes protected, more often abandoned. None, however, provides greater aesthetic delight or more effectively provokes speculation about a person and a way of life than the tomb of Jamali–Kamali—one of Delhi's great, but least known treasures.

Pages 20–21
Tomb of Jamali–Kamali—the ceiling of the tomb chamber

Notes

1 See references by Simon Digby in Rosemary Crill, Susan Stronge, and Andrew Topsfield, eds., *Arts of Mughal India—Studies in Honour of Robert Skelton,* London: Victoria and Albert Museum and Ahmedabad, Mapin Publishing, 2004, 19, fn. 5.

2 *The Travels of Ibn Battuta, A.D. 1325–1354,* Cambridge: Hakluyt Society, 1971, III: 625.

3 'Abdu-I-Qadir ibn-i-Muluk Shah al-Badaoni, *Muntakhabu-i-Tawarikh,* transl. and ed. George S.A. Ranking, Patna: Academica Asiatica, 1973 (reprint), I: 411.

4 For a brief discussion of Jamali's life and further references, see Jamali-yi Dihlawi, *The Mirror of Meanings,* trans. A. A. Seyed-Gohrab, Costa Mesa, CA: Mazda Publishers, 2002, xi–xvii. The book is otherwise a translation and discussion of Jamali's *Mirt ai-Ma'ani,* a poetic expression of Sufism.

5 'Abdu-I-Qadir ibn-i-Muluk Shah al-Badaoni, op. cit, I: 429–430.

6 *Ibid.*

7 Zahiruddin Muhammad Babur, *The Baburnama—Memoirs of Babur, Prince and Emperor,* trans. and ed. Wheeler M. Thackston, Washington, D.C.: Freer Gallery of Art and Arthur M. Sackler Gallery, 1996, 373.

8 Ibid., 433.

9 Nawwab Samsam-ud-Daula Shah Nawaz Khan and 'Abdul Hayy, *The Maathirul-Umara,* Patna: Janaki Prakashan, 1979 (reprint), I; 568–569, which includes information on Jamali within a short biography of his son Shaikh Gadai Kambu.

10 Carr Stephens, *Archaeology and Monumental Remains of Delhi,* Allahabad: Kitab Mahal, 1967 (reprint), 171–3. (This date is repeated in the exhaustive two-volume study by INTACH, *Delhi—The Built Heritage: A Listing,* Delhi: Indian National Trust for Culture and Architectural Heritage, 1999, II: 312.)

11 G.H.R. Tillotson, *Mughal India,* San Francisco: Chronicle Books, 1990, 35–6. For further references to this monument, as well as important discussions of Mughal architecture in general, see: Ebba Koch, *Mughal Architecture,* Munich: Prestel, 1991, and Catherine B. Asher, *The New Cambridge History of India—Architecture of Mughal India,* Cambridge: Cambridge University Press, 1992.

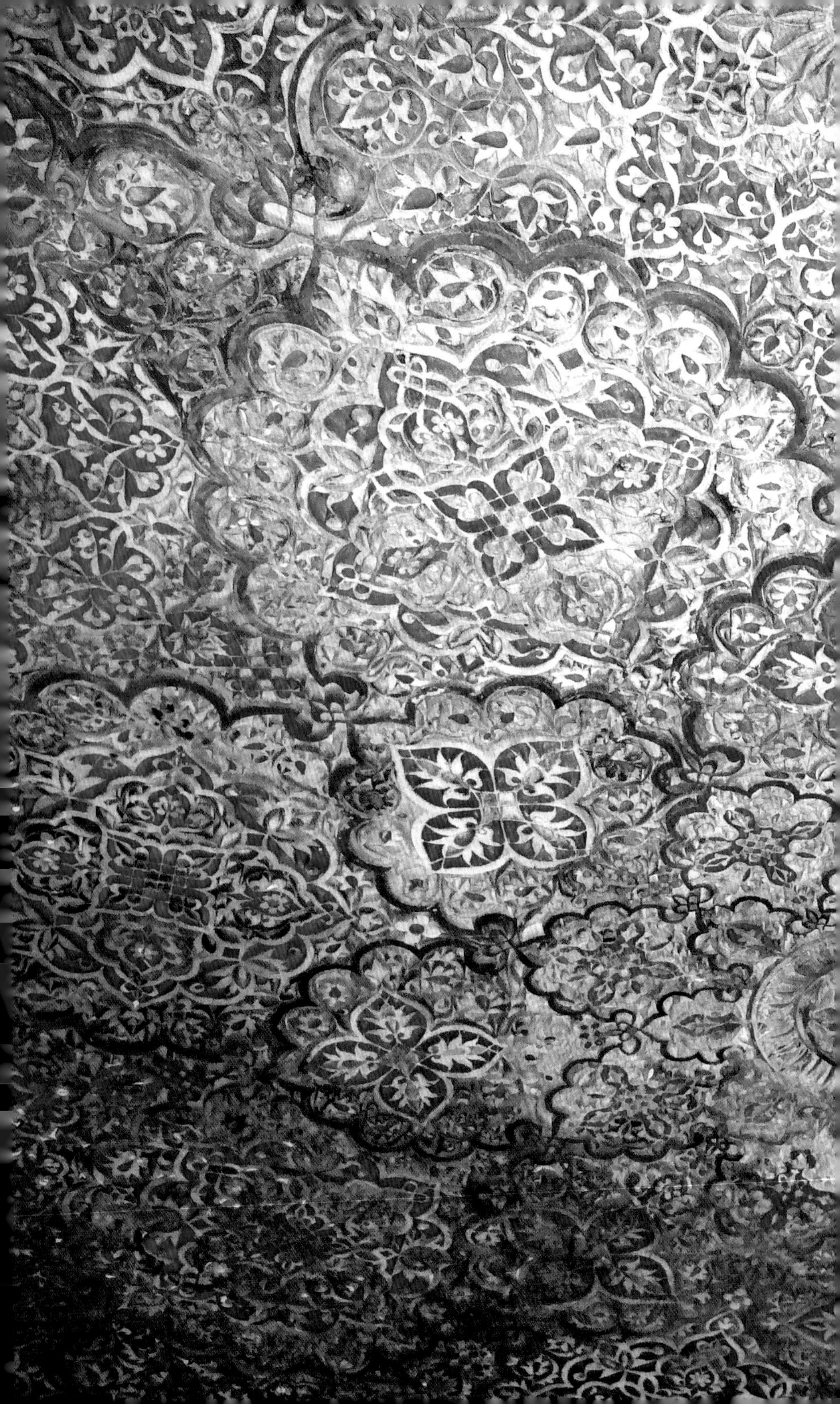

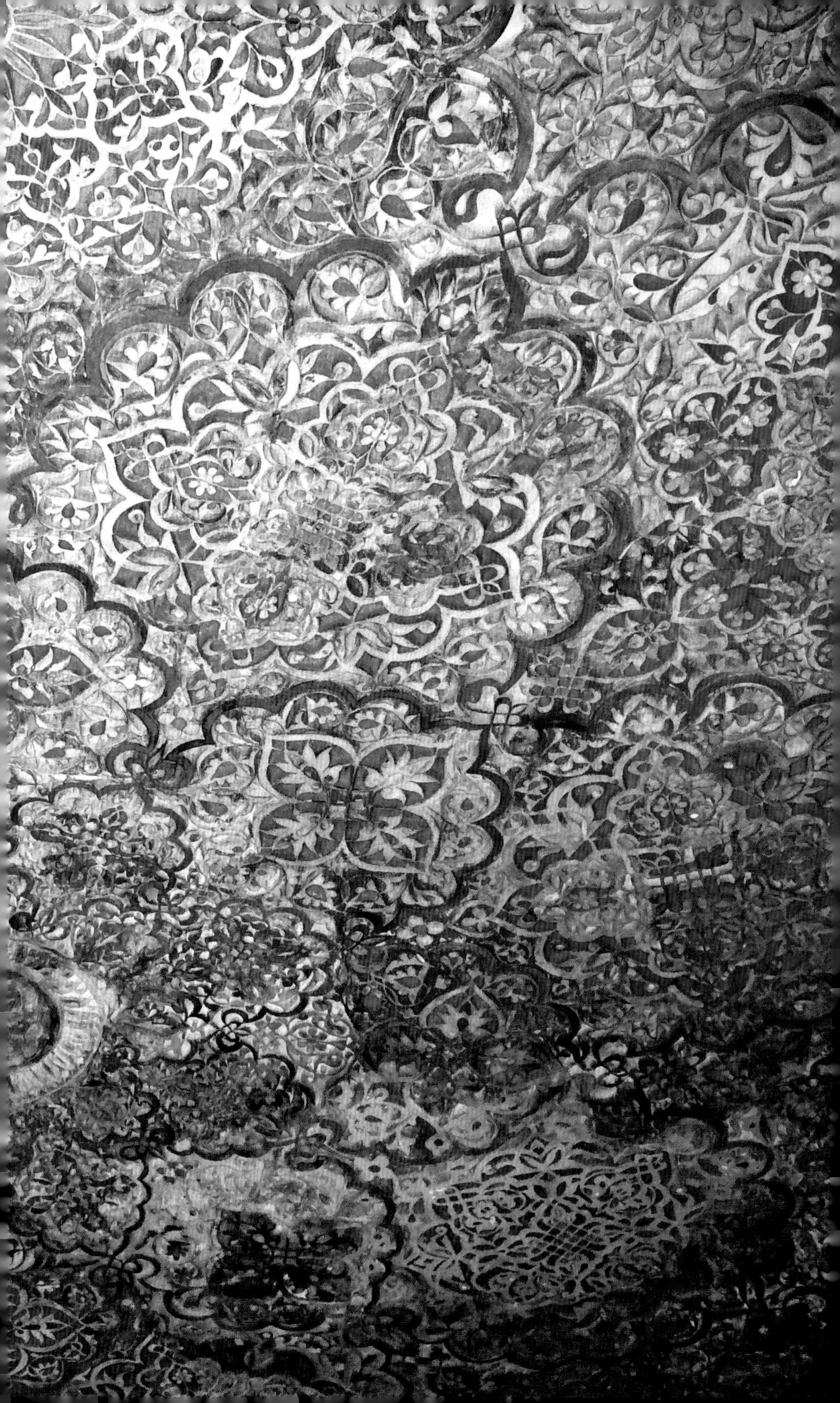

Part One

Just off busy Mehrauli-Gurgaon Road in Delhi, India, the sixteenth-century Sufi court poet Jamali is buried in a tomb next to Kamali, of whom the printed matter says "identity unknown", but who helpful guides say, according to oral tradition, was the poet's lover. Little about them is known.

In the plump dusk, I hear
a peacock screech,
eye marks on my lover's neck.

Kamali, let's go
to the lake
to moisten our love scars.

I will wash mud from
your muscled legs.

My secrets rest
in the wedding
hut. I visit another
man as the moon
circles down.

Come my protégé,
my Kamali, to bed.
I will show you
moves of a new
planet as no
astrologer could.

Bonfires blaze
in Delhi's winter.
While dogs howl
I remove your kurta,
your trousers, to teach
you pyrotechnics.
I am not called Professor
of Fire for naught.

The donkey is caught
between two worlds, as
am I, as are you.
Last night I dreamt of two
princes at play.
Vehicles passing both ways
will praise our marble tomb.

When we were boys
I watched you draw
under the shade of
the champa.

I watched you
in the forest
as you herded
goats, twenty,
thirty of them,
maybe even more,
prancing behind you
as I wished to.

Under the eyelash moon,
I watched you gaze
skyward. Will I ever
take you and when,
I wondered.

Rehearsing for us,
I watched the kingfisher
consume the lizard.

The grass green male
parrot sports a dark
pink collar.
I have ordered the stitchers
to sew one for us, each.

At cow dust hour,
meet me in the orchard.

Like birds, we'll raid
the neighbour's guava trees.

Our hidden
ravishments roil
inside. I see your
sister, a new bride,
chirping with
pleasure. How long can
we go on like this?

Pleasure-making
couples parade
the fog-laden streets.
I long for you,
lowing with grief.

Kamali, where have you gone?
Have you told our secret?
Let's meet by the stream
near the bamboo grove.

Bonfires burn
on every street.
One day I will
startle you,
circle you, as you huddle
for warmth,
to show all our attachment.

When you watch me dance
with the marigold clad
beauty of our town,
do not grieve my boy,
it is you I am picturing.

It is you who will
be buried with me
in twin marble graves
high on the hill.

It will be too late
for any to object.
Let them say
what they will.
And for centuries, if they want.

Tonight the boatman will
row us to the island where
he has fixed
a feast and a bed
so soft, my friend,
we will never be the same.

Our secret is safe
with him.
I paid him in sapphires.

Tomorrow I must go
to far-off lands,
leave my winter quarters,
carry the spice-box
south.

Young men
with brooms
brush away the plumeria leaves.
Such sweeping will go on
when I am gone.

For sport,
watch the wiry mason
collect water in the
central well. How he
descends the stairs
with his pitcher,
then flies up.

Do not speak with him.
I beg you.

When men brush the warming ground,
do they sweep the
serpent spirits out too?
Dust plumes up into the hot air.

Do you hear the steps now
of my uncle's prize horse?
It is nearing time to part.
Fog falls through my loins.
Like a pubescent girl, I hanker
for your chest, lost.

Look! The field is
filled with white cranes,
migrating witnesses to our lust.

Kamali you anger me.
Go. The men will give
you a broom. Sweep
the sagwan leaves
from my courtyard.
Join the roomboys.

Your moaning is of no use.

Take heed.
I have my eye on the young
mason, his onyx eyes.
His lengthy fingers
will do me good.

I shall shatter
the tiles of heaven
to illustrate how
you peeve me.
A pile of red and blue shards.

My love for you
and hate are large.
One day I consume you,
the next,
regurgitate.

And you?
You seem to waver, as well.

Nights filled with massive
thunderbolts, dreams of rival
women and men.

Violet sky, blue doors,
green on the girls' attire—
all praise Delhi's colours.
Your lovemoves pale the palette.

In the humid fields, our odd audience:
a tiger here, a squirrel there.
Cheetahs, too, appear curious.

You say, Kamali, you dreamt
of bolts of velvet,
carmine clothes for us
both. Does this portend
good luck?

Who is the peacock
here? One day you are,
then me.
I love our shifting
plumage, also
how the peafowl
guard us from intruders.

What happened?
Like a serpent eagle
attacked, I am featherless.
Your fierceness, Kamali,
is catastrophic.

Your smooth royal fingers,
your rajah-like stance, bore me.
Seasons aiding the goatherd,
your practiced milking hands,
your humbleness I love.

Tonight you must do
as I say. Dress
as my bride. I will walk
through Delhi's streets
with you unafraid.

Then I will regale you
with rubies.
Camphor, aloe wood
will perfume our tent.
No amount of liquor
could make us so drunk.
I promise.

Your sisters watch you,
I can see.

Monsoon winds
hurl the buttresses,
wind chimes
crack to smithereens,
I surrender order.
Take me in your arms.

You drain my plan
to go off with the others,
mount my horse.
I am like a small child.

Kamali, I must leave tomorrow
and you must stay.

Turn over.
I will take you now.
Our love calls will
inflame god and goddess alike.

You said you told that girl in the red sari
go home to your mother.
Please tell the one in turquoise too.

Ah! I heard you carousing.
The soaking courtyard let loose
with laughter.
Do the roomboys
ply you with wine?
Do others know
your serpentine beauty?

The slave king Balban
has his fine tomb.
Who will see our
monuments to love
when we are gone?
What will they say?
You were my wife?

Down the hill,
goats roam the muddy streets.
A girl walks two monkeys on a leash.

It is time, my student,
you learned
the songs of birds:
paradise flycatcher,
the grey hornbill.

After the hysterical rain,
the streaked laughing thrush
claims his turf again.
Kamali Kamali I sing
as I claim mine.

Are you keeping
something from me?
Have you entered
private palaces before?

Fortified walls
do not compare
to your fortified face.
Go now.
I have lost patience.

You say I tire you?
You tire me.

Pillars, cloisters,
floods everywhere,
parapets, moats—
I don't care.

Mausoleum, mosque, tomb too.

I don't know what to make of this.

Gossipers tell
of snakes with beards—
milk, the only way
to appease them.

If we go on,
they will cart me
to the madhouse.
Your legs, for example,
make me insane.

No night is long enough,
no season, no year.
We have come to
another winter in Delhi and
I drive with desire, still.

The hunt begins tomorrow.
I shall go. You stay
and tend the court.
With every stab to leopard
or fox, I lose verve.

Is it the fog?
Wind rocks the jacaranda.
Again, bonfires burn.
Your body cocks the world
out of focus.

I am torn.

A donkey on the road.
An elephant.
My friends together.
Trout from the
northern hills.
The Yamuna.
Nothing interests me.

A battered statue
by the mosque.
Two feet remain,
the rest is dust.

Did you see the slobbering
puppy? Its mother killed
a peacock
as I would, for you.

Never able to share a table,
what will become of us?

I have left you a letter
regarding this
in the niche at Balban's tomb,
the ink, a sea of illegibleness.

Like a prisoner,
one arm gone,
then the other,

I am injured.
Kamali, you ask me why,
your brow a map of wondering.
For you silly man, this putrid
pail of sorrow.

Feverish,
I must take to bed.
My face, my buttocks burn.
I say, ban the arsonist.

A squirrel peers
into my doorway,
sees this clump
of man.

The men wear red shawls
and blue turbans today.
A sea of hues crash.

Again, an orange fog has come.
Where have you been, Kamali,
are you a whoremonger?

Why is your head
always in my books?
Storms are heading south
from the Himalayas.
Gather your belongings,
we will do some travelling.

Tonight we will study maps
by the light of my oil lamp,
to educate you
in more ways than one.

I ordered the kheer
drugged with love potions.
Have some.

On the map of your body, there is
nowhere I would not travel.

Part Two

Throughout the reigns of Sikandar Lodi, Babur and Humayun, Jamali's travels take him to Syria, Iran, Baghdad, Ceylon, Mecca, Herat, Damascus, Palestine and Spain, making for many separations.

Hot wind blasted my torso
with dust as I left Delhi
reeking of beauty.
Stunned by my zeal for you,

I passed a junkheap:
terracotta horse head,
clay arm near a bush.
I slept in a field

of gaillardia, red-streaked
like pixie flame.
"What is this place?"
I quizzed a peahen.

Dragonflies seemed to listen.
Before our bond, Kamali,
I pitched into motion.

In the stinging sky,
I rode on to Gujarat,
eyes on the windy horizon,
the smacking smell of dulse,
gulls crisscrossing the universe.

I sailed south to Ceylon,
the indigo sky adrift with stars,
a luminous tomb roof.
Three days from land
as I ruminated on lovers' tombs,
a mountain came in view.

Through the jungle, I rode
toward Adam's Peak.
Fat leeches wrapped
round my ankles,
thrived in the rank green.

Under a great, strange tree
an elephant suckled her newborn
near a turquoise pond.
Lime leaves flapped down.

Rubies glittered
off the river sand
at Ratnapura,
the peak's steep side.
All I pictured was
your butterfly laugh,
your glittering eyes.

Clad in rags, fingers jammed,
I started up the cliff's sheer face.

Overshadower of sky and tide,
Kamali, I yearned to woo you more
the higher I climbed.
They say the Peak
is forty miles beneath Paradise.

Wrapped in bear hides,
gummy with ash,
I traipsed on as qalandar.

Dumbfounded, I sat
at the tables of poets,
lay skins on their floors.

To their sense, I spoke nonsense,
unhitched their speech.

They relayed stories,
as I whirled round their rooms.

I gagged on roast camel,
downed bugalamun with zest.

Alien lands, alien food!
my home routine gone—
my own dal, my own chapati,
horse manure, jasmine.

On the mats of strangers
retching from date liquor,
sick for home.

Such longing was a million
times nothing
compared to no you.
Swathed in fever,
my heart pumped water
rather than red life,
my lips logey as wet cloth.

As I sleep in your arms now,
all this long ago,
you lassoo me in my dreams.
Your tresses
are making me nervous.

Why are you growing
your locks longer and longer?

Remember how I studied
the ropes and snares of hunters,
remember when I was barely grown,
I shared opium
with long-haired ruffians?

Once the sky
turned a pink so glaring,
a sign,
I vowed to live a clean life.

But wisdom won—
I rode on
with the cup-bearers again.

Tramps practice love
on man, woman, beast.
Their nights know no measure.
Days: rest, recover.
Avoid war, conserve love power.

After a storm one day
I lay on the sand
as sailors repaired our hull,
dreaming of times past.

A beardless boy loved me
in a fervour so wild,
the gusty tent seemed on fire.

You, Kamali—I had to have you.

Now, we're here—
tonight I must write a poem
to praise King Babur.
Then let us don the pink panelled
skirts of dervishes
and disappear.

Moonrise, I make
my way to your bed.

As we collide,
sparks turn night to noon.

No rains deluge like you,
no breeze like your breath.

I didn't know I knew
your moves—

then, in a mirror, I saw
you raise your arm,

stir the air,
how—wait—

be still—lie down,
no need to move now.

Light starts to crack apart
the navy sky.

Our staffs hail the air.
Moonset—dash home to my wife.

Sometimes you soar through fog,
a low bird.

You appear from the mist,
then you are gone.

Your face is a field
of light. The denseness,

no veil to vision.
Nothing can pale your plumage.

Wind breezing air, weather!
The wide-faced sea is for me.

But an inland room even more—
you, me and debauchery.

I ponder the Masters, stand on my head,
stumble about like a mute.

I do not mock those who
celebrate grand boulevards

to Heaven—thigh, face, neck.
Why, though, elaborate what is plain?

Genitalia and anus lead nowhere.
Love stops short in their presence.

Today Kamali—a lesson
in meteorology.
Fog moves across
the screen of sky.

P'teer, p'teer, p'teer.
The Plaintive Cuckoo
disappears.
The mist, a canvas for you.

Black fog obscures ceiling,
east, west, floor.
Am I standing on my head?
I love you more and more.

Let's play cards tonight.
Who will win, who will lose?
Afterwards, "fetch the ropes"
one of us will say.
Our bond will pump God's blood.

Why are you going North?
Is the answer, Kamali, unspeakable?
Are we shipwrecked?

The Masters think
love kills disease.
When I can't have you,
I am sick.

I am crazed.
I am speaking with animals,
eating grass.

I am wearing hooves on my feet,
I dance a Khattak to charm the beasts.

"Fishy," I say when I come to a pond,
"we have much to discuss about love."

Fog covered berry and bush,
settled on the tamarinds.

Ghostlike and slow,
a shade strolled
across the mango orchard.
The mass paused,
looked to be a bear
on hind legs.

"That is Kamali,
your friend,"
someone snickered.

When the figure moved,
I knew you were home.

Is it shadows you love?
Let's go to the yard.
Tell me everything, Lovebird.

While you were gone,
I feasted at the King's table.
Mirror-like fish slid down my throat.

Under canopies, with ambassadors,
I dined with Uzbeks and Qizilbashes,
loose grass screens cooling us.

Men inflamed elephants, prodded camels.
To amuse us, the beasts fought.

Wrestlers jabbed as acrobats twirled aloft,
daggers and sable wraps were given to guests.
Piles of purses and piles of gold
were given to Babur first.

Did you know he wrote
the story of his life?
Humanyun read the pages.
King Babur loved a boy in his youth.

The teasing strapping boy of long ago
bound my limbs to posts,
loved me from behind.
The rain roared…
it was monsoon time.

Kamali, you tell me a story now.

Let us bend towards God,
unpack the ropes.

You will lose the need to move…
Coo-rooroo-rooroo…
You will turn untame,
stretching, rustling,
ringing with a broad
tenor as court musicians
play the bansari!

We will sponge, soap, and swab.
"Roomboy! Douse us with coco balm!"

Coo-rooroo-rooroo—
on the ground this morning
the Panduk courted.

The male Dove
hopped towards
the female's rear.
Motionless, her back to him.
He swelled his feathers,
she flit hers.

Coo-rooroo-rooroo.
He mounted her.
They took their time.

Time to stop moving—
no run, no shift, no glide,
no unquiet from morning to night.

Kamali. Let's stagger towards the paradise of calm.

Part Three

Jamali reminisces to Kamali about the time when Jamali had returned from a hunt and a battle in Mewat, where he had been sent by the Mughal king, Babur.

The sand blew so hard—remember?
We had to take cover.

"How close was the lion?"
you asked.

"Take off your turban,"
I said.

Outside, torn roses blew past.
Butterflies scattered.

Remember how the roof tiles
shook with pleasure?

"How close was the lion?"
you asked again.

My mind roamed to that long ago dusk.
A smokey-eyed boy poled his boat down the Indus.

Later, camped in a tent,
I slept unclothed, alone.

Through the night, I rode a black leopard's lean back,
my privates abuzz in the oleander air.

"The lion was close," I said.

Battle blood from the day before.
A tender boy bled from an arrow strike.

I covered him in my kurta as he died.
Sickened, I rode into the overlit noon,

came on a field of riderless elephants
crazed from gun sound, their soldiers trampled,

common death, everywhere I looked. Before this,
I was sick for you, and home too—now, nothing at all.

I taste apple on your mouth, Kamali,
smell wheat on your chest—you have been threshing!

Winds of the earth fatigue and seas find rest,
the sad, bloody hunts of war and beast recede.

The lion was so close,
I felt his unusual breath.

From all sides, we stabbed the beast.
I saw the lion's heart—his and the soldier boy's,

the same—furrows, auricles, vena cavas, twists,
turns, astounding aortas. After this, how to find life again!

Kamali, love equals life, as man's and lion's hearts do.
I knew then, you are my life, my love, my lion, my wife.

I journeyed feverish across serpent-filled underbrush,
through monsoon-flooded gullies, made my way

from tomb of this one to tomb of that, then out on the sea
one night, I made a pact with the devilish waves:

for centuries, Jamali and Kamali will rest in graves
inches apart for all to witness.

Tamerlane and Ghenghis Khan run through King Babur's
blooded veins, but he has a softer side. "Babur,"

I will say, "build a tomb for love of man by man,
as natural as your conquering strain, like any beast's

heartbeat, like the sun coming up." I looked about and
there were stones, so many large boulders of those here

then gone. Straw huts newly appeared one day in a field—
deserted, the next, as Hindus moved along…

What is this looseness to home?
Home moves with one, when there is love.

Our home, Kamali, will be high on a Delhi hill,
our bed, white marble tombs.

What has my life been?
I moved as beggar,
as dervish I danced,
wrote verses,
fathered sons,
hunted, battled,
stumbled as tavern straggler,
skinned my knees,
heard a cheetah call,
too dark, too scared, to set up camp,
food finally for the wolves.

I sailed oceans,
I prayed,
watched as the king was given a diamond
worth all the world's commerce of half a day,
and yet as I saw that boy die,
life lacked sense. I beg you now,
Kamali, please speak up—
your silence is slaying me.

Trees high on both sides, up
the only way to go,
up the mountain pass.
Sheer incline
heaves down the
rocky cliff.

Chimes ticking the air, and flutes:
commotion on the plateaus.
Faces of dark men
painted as white birds.
In peacock-feather skirts,
they dance.

The alchemous fog falls
fast on the scene.
I stray into the ancient woods
with my soon-to-be-dead father,
hunt leopards together...
drumbeat.

Dusk's pink threads weave into night.
Shaken, alone with the beasts,
thoughts of your flesh,
I ponder the conquering heart's core:
battles, sexual takings
and leavings, predators.

What is love, what is natural?

I pulse through this hourglass world,
tempo of sand fall,
move my boney feet up the pass,
move memory over this planetary surface,
trace of all gone before, and what's to be,
the past shivering alive into now.

Blood pulses through me,
as I pulse through the world,
constant from my black curls
to my brown toes. Up in a tree,
the leopard's yellow eyes light
the lightless night. To myself I say,

Don't be afraid, my boy! When my boyish body
tagged after the goatherd, hoping for a glimpse of you—
men and men! My body holds what I was and am—
know it or not—same heart now, same heart then,
slithering oily from my mother's womb, out
into earth's fragrant wind.

My long song comes as sand drops
down the hourglass.

Lion, I call you *lion*.
Your eyes, for one.

Your glowering, sundrenched torso,
your muscled thighs,

bronze arms. When you
stretch your arms

towards me, throw your garments
to the floor, recline

on plush cushions, lay
down your sword,

wait, gaze and wait,
time done with…

no battle, nor woods,
nor outdoors at all.

Yesterday the hour sounded, Lion,
sand descended,

how many years now
me and my wild night lion

moan, glisten, growl?
Who says there's no time

in the beamish fog,
no wolf, no colour, no cat,

and here comes nothing like a man.

A dervish?
How mistaken one could be!

A man?
A lion?
A woman?

Before Babur, before Humayun,
one long winter ago,
Sultan Sikandar, the ruler,
himself a poet and poet-lover,
crowned me poet of the court.

When he died, Lodi, his son,
had many of his father's men
killed off.
I feared death then, or jail.

Snows outside threaten now,
and fear returns.
Inside with you, Kamali, coals.
Rooms with beds swell to world size.

As you sleep,
I guard your limbs,
your chest's heat,
fur of my prize lion.

I am yours as dervish or saint,
in sickness, in health.
I am yours in battle,
or in the thick forest of the hunt.

Out where the hunt happens,
men converge around the lion,
maul the thing, cold light could
strike, thunder approach
and no thing would dampen the kill.

Threat of hunt,
threat of battle,
threat of some lockup.

I have lost sight of nature, and danger
lurks over every hill.

I dread night, jerk awake.

My breeches stink up the room.

When I hear footfalls,
my dumb heart scrapes:

Pear
Noose
Rose petal

Do crows migrate?

Will men cart me off to jail?

You said you once saw an indigo bird—remember Kamali?—
off-course, like me, in a Delhi garden,
perched on the raggedy cosmos.

Imagine ambling free
between narrow cliffs,
forms like tent whirls
making rookeries.

I can see you crouching on the banks of the Yamuna,
hands under water, ready to clutch the fish.
I see you at the stove, cooking biryani.

Confinement smothers me
like a hellhole.

To picture you is a huge wound.
I refuse tears, not to lose fluid.

Gems came my way,
saffron robes, glorious turbans.
I rode in ivory-covered palanquins,
covered you with purple shawls,
bound you with silken bonds.
My underarm stench now thrills the horseflies,
birds, a lost cause.

To think, you cooked me rice!
To think, your fingers outlined my lips.

Is it snowing?

Oh! delicate powder...
how to breathe if not for picturing.

My mind is paradise,
as time seeps from me.

I hear a bumblebee.

Through my mind's hall,
skulls reek.

I'm the sea.

Remember, Kamali, how snow piled high on Himalayan peaks?

The lion was close,
her footprints showed.

The brush of her coat
spun gold in the sun.

The relaxed lion sunned herself
near the watering hole.

The sundial keeps moving—

Man is wolf to man, a sadhu said—
and the sky—it must be turning red.

Part Four

It is 1536, the Mughal ruler Humayun is in power. Jamali has gone west to Gujarat with Humayun and other warriors, to conquer territory. Kamali speaks.

Through the difficult
air, Jamali,
I speak to you
from afar.

Months have passed.
Still it is you
on the paths,

in the fields.
Your face,
I crave.

The shine
of your black
eyes pulls me

by heat
so fractious and deep
I can't stand straight.

Rattled birds
dart and hit
the frantic air.

I keep seeing a
man's face
on the path

near the bamboo grove.
Hollow cheeks,
taut.

Barefoot
in the branch,
the heart at last.

Wordless Jamali,
do not ask.

Sadness soaks me.

Meager speech.
Blankness—
rash.

In this thicket—
Dragonfly,
take heed.

Your face—sweet
beautyscar
alight.

Jamali, your face…
I'm speechless.
No.

Your eyes are
deep. No.

Words land
loud on the
persimmon tree.

Mouth.
Hip.

I cower.
Words blow like wind.

I cower, Jamali!

I'm chopping wood.

I'm going
to chop
saplings.

I taught you weather,
Jamali, and
fog.

I taught you
Great Bear
in the sky,

monsoon—
words
you thought
you knew, I
made fresh.

Then you left.

Birds
sang
single notes.

You have
warred
too much, my

Professor
of peafowl, my

guide
through the palace
of pleasure:

arch
bridge
corridor.

Banners swelling light
as we loved beneath.

Your muskpod—
I need
to smell
your chest.

I can't say
Jamali, remember
to fuel our loving.

Once I told you
of the slight crease
below one lover's waist, how
from his navel to his genitals,
soft hair made arrows.

Remember the costumed boy,
cheeks a rush of rose,
and lithe, how
fiendishly he danced
to the lutes,
his feet never still.
I took him to bed,
found he was a girl!

And remember Jamali
that bristly
old man,
scratching his buttocks?

Squatting on the terrace,
slurping his dal,
he looked up
so kindly,
my heart pumped sugar.

You said
Kamali
will we reach
this lustre?

Soon after, you mounted
your war-adorned elephant,
raised a red triangle flag
and disappeared.

Nights now
sleepless.

Gulping water.
Tuk tuk tuk—the owl.

I am dismantled
like glass chips.

You were
the one
who twirled
to pieces.

You,
making your way
through the desert
subject to enemy
and beast.

You are on a pass—
enemy troops
lust for your
heart.

And I
do nothing,
safe in my tent,

a paralyzed pasban
against time
and dark.

In my sleep,
I ride
a giant peacock,
a snake in its mouth.

My dead mother
was a dyer of cloth.

Madder, ochre,
alizarin—
breath of wild spice.

Billowing cotton
hung in the wind,
pink dye
dripped to the ground.

I'd never,
I thought,
see beauty
equal to
that wet colour

until you,
my Shaykh.

From afar,
your sandals removed,
I watched you
run turbanless
through the rose grove,
loose curls
swirling behind.

Your strong back,
head erect,
your long, delineated spine…

I craved you'd want me,
spend your spinning mind
on mine.

The air is
filling
with elephant dung,
waking me up.

Curly, black clouds
are circling
the fat, fiery moon.

Drumming.
A horse skids.
Someone here.
Someone's in my tent.

Jamali murda.

Jamali is dead.

I'm scratching
the ground,
breathing dirt.
No sky, no star,
only down.

I'll murder
the astronomers.
Keep them away.

Jamali!
You went out
the second door
of the inn!

They are
carting you
home.

Peafowl stumble,
severed
from each other—
no—
they search.

Velvet-saddled horses
come in view.

Thirty or so.

Smokiness.

The horses slow down.

A man says
"Jamali murda."

Who
am
I
talking
to?

"Elephants will follow
carrying Shaykh Jamali."

Oh.

Pale yellow petals
pile up by my tent.

People offer apricots.

The tomb, ready.

Birds and drums lamenting.

I want
to sleep next
to your corpse.

You, bathed
of battle blood,
me robbed—
neither bather,
nor soaper.

You washed mud
from my legs once.

I turn the cot-bed
upside down,

throw the tray,
heave the mirror at the stone.

No more
will I
throw my arm
over your bony hip
as you dream,
hold your member
in my palm.

No more
will I glare
at your face
as you babble
nonsense.

No more winter spats,
no more song.

The horseman lifts
the crimson cotton shroud—
my Shaykh
made small by death.

Jingle of bell.

His shriveling
shell, a piece
of small flesh.
Jamali—you were tall.

Riderless, the sour
old elephant
hauls you.

The tomb, laden
with jasmine and sweets.

Masters prepare
their dance.
Hubbub of
ney,
cauldrons of
fruit
and rice,

the courtyard, full.

You, released
from your body's
jail, villagers feast,
your spirit, free.

No.

Your forehead is gone.
Your eyes are gone.
Gone your cheeks,
your neck.
Gone your chest.

Gone hips,
buttocks, penis.
No more legs.

Your hair—gone.
Your words!
Gone is your voice,
your whisper.

A pubic hair
of yours,
found
in your
bed—this
is my wealth now.

Your tomb—no, our tomb—gleams,
polished red and blue tiles,
white marble graves
buffed to a shine.

Roomboys who brought us
love potions, make
death preparations.

Flute players
line the dust-blown path
to the mosque,

stinging of celebration.
In every niche, candles wavering.

Through the ascending crowd,
I wander down towards mute Delhi.

Pricker bushes brush my legs.
Nightingales lose their song.

I thought you'd come to me in dream but you don't.

Leaves on the champa, like torn cloth,
the sky, pink satin,
the ground, linen.
The world, like dyed cloth I will never touch.

Jamali murda.

The jealous hill has you now.

Your sound recedes.

My hands
you loved—
idle now.

I bury my pen
and charcoal
in the ground.

Jamali murda.

I visit the bamboo grove
where we used to meet
by the stream.

Jamali murda,
the mango orchard too.

White cranes
look
for you.

I am sinking.

Birds stream uphill
as I go down.

Goodbye hibiscus.
Goodbye plumeria.

Snow must be falling on the Himalayas.

Wrapped in shawls,
a lemon in my mouth,
I am walking north.

Notes

p. 24 **kurta** A loose-fitting tunic or shirt, knee-length or longer.

p. 31 **Balban** The founder of the Slave Dynasty, Balban was the Sultan of Delhi from 1265 to 1290. His dilapidated tomb, very near the Jamali–Kamali Tomb, was the first time a true arch was used for support in an Indian structure.

p. 33 **Yamuna** The Yamuna, or Jumna, is the second-most sacred river in India, after the Ganges (Ganga). It begins in a frozen lake and glacier in the Himalayas, and flows for 850 miles, past Delhi, past the Taj Mahal in Agra, southeast to the Ganges River.

p. 35 **kheer** Pudding made with basmati rice, milk, sugar, cardamom, ground almonds and saffron.

p. 38 **Adam's Peak** A mountain in Sri Lanka, formerly Ceylon, sacred to Muslims, Hindus, Buddhists, and Christians. For over a thousand years travellers, including Marco Polo, have made pilgrimages to the peak to see the indentation of what looks like a giant footprint, thought to be put there by Adam, the Buddha, Shiva, or St. Thomas, depending on the religion.

p. 38 **qalandar** An itinerant Sufi, who learns and teaches during his travels, and who partakes of intoxicants. Qalandars whirl, dance and utter refrains while performing rituals. The 11th century Sufi Baba Tahir wrote:

I am the mystic gypsy called Qalandar /I have neither fire, home, nor monastery./ By day I wander about the world, and at night/ I sleep with a brick under my head.

p. 39 **bugalamun** Means *turkey* in modern Persian. In the *Baburnama,* Babur refers to this bird as having *"delicious flesh. In winter it descends to the mountain foothills, and if it is made to fly over a vineyard, it cannot fly anymore and can be caught."*

p. 39 **tresses** In *The Mirror of Meanings,* Jamali explores in verse how parts of the body relate to God, according to the Sufis.

Every step on the road of the tresses is narrow;
the world of the tresses is the world of darkness.

p. 43 **Khattak** A traditional fast-tempoed dance, requiring physical skill and performed with zeal.

p. 44 The *Baburnama* tells of Babur's youthful, sexual love for a boy. His son, Humayun, did read his father's memoirs.

p. 45 **bansari** One of the earliest wind instruments. Seven round holes are bored in a hollow piece of bamboo stick. Some bansari are held straight away from the face while others are held transversely, parallel to the eyebrows as it was used by Lord Krishna.

p. 49 **Tamerlane and Ghenghis Khan** Ancestors of Babur. The fifth generation on his father's side was Tamerlane and the fifteenth "degree" from Genghis Khan on his mother's side.

p. 50 **diamond** Thought by many to be the Koh-i-noor diamond. From the *Baburnama*:
"When Humayun got to Agra, the people of Bikramajit's clan were thinking of fleeing, but the men Humayun had stationed there seized them and held them under guard. Humayun did not let them be plundered, and by their own agreement they presented Humayun with many jewels and gems, among which was a famous diamond Sultan Alauddin had acquired. It is well known that a gem merchant once assessed its worth at the whole world's expenditure for half a day. It must weigh eight mithcals. When I came, Humayun presented it to me, but I gave it right back to him."

p. 54 **palanquin** An ornately decorated covered litter, carried on poles on the shoulders of two to six men. Sometimes singers or storytellers entertained the luxurious travellers.

p. 55 **man is a wolf to man** Plautus, a soldier, a wanderer, and ancient Rome's (c. 254 BCE) most renowned playwright, said *homo homini lupus.*

p. 62 **pasban** Persian for the word *watchman.*

p. 63 **shaykh** Persian word indicating respect for Sufi masters. Also spelt as 'sheikh' and 'shaikh'.

p. 64 **second door of the inn** The world is The Inn of Two Doors, according to the Sufis. We enter through the first door, Birth, and leave via the second, i.e. Death.

p. 67 **ney** Likely the first pitched instrument. It is an oblique rim blown reed flute with five finger holes in front and one thumb hole in the back.

p. 67 **body's jail** In the later thirteenth century, Rumi, the Persian Sufi poet, introduced music and dancing during the funeral rites. He wrote:
"When the human spirit, after years of imprisonment in the cage and dungeon of the body, is at length set free, and wings its flight to the Source whence it came, is not this an occasion for rejoicings, and thanks, and dancing?"

Jamali and Kamali

Jamali was a Sufi poet, born in Delhi in 1483. An insatiable traveller, he spent years journeying through Central Asia and went as far as Spain and Jerusalem, visiting and collecting stories from Sufi mystics and poets. Jamali was also known as Shaikh Hamid bin Fazlullah, Dervish Jamali Kanbo Dihlawi, and Jamali-yi Dihlawi. As a young man, his name was changed from *Jalali* (meaning awe-inspiring) to *Jamali* (meaning lovable or beauty-inspiring). Jamali was a follower of Shaikh Sama al-din, who some say was his father-in-law, his uncle, and/or the father of a close friend. Jamali fathered three sons.

He wrote *Mirror of Meanings* (*Mir'at al-Ma'ani*), a book-length poem, about how the erotic is linked to God in Sufi thought, and *The Sun and the Moon (Mihr u Mah),* an allegorical romance. Jamali's *Spiritual Journey of the Mystics* (*Sayr al-'Arifin*) is his biography of 14 Indian mystics. In the book, he also relates several personal stories: how he had telepathic contact and a close friendship with a young man who lived in the forest and ate leaves, how he was cured of loss of appetite by a Bengali doctor who gave him mercury-pills and how his teacher told him that the heat of love is enough to drive out disease. Jamali indulged in night-time devotions, involving straps and ropes.

When Jamali returned to India, he became a mentor and friend of the ruler Sultan Sikandar Lodi, also a poet. Jamali was named Poet Laureate, literally 'king of poets', in Sikandar's court. When Sikandar's son, Sultan Ibrahim

Lodi, took over in 1517, he was brutal with his father's favourites, although Jamali remained unharmed.

Babur, the first Mughal ruler, conquered India in 1526. He came to favour Jamali. Babur's memoir, *The Baburnama,* mentions that he sent Jamali into battle twice and invited him to a large celebration in Agra. Under Babur, in 1528, the Jamali–Kamali Mosque and Tomb began to be constructed, and was completed during the reign of Babur's son, Humayun. In that era, it was unusual to build a tomb for a living person. Jamali went to Gujarat with Humayun in 1536, where he was killed in battle. In a rare act, his body was transported back to Delhi for burial.

No one knows who Kamali was. According to Delhi's oral tradition, he was Jamali's homosexual lover. Others believe he never existed and that *Kamali* is simply a play on the word *Jamali,* or was Jamali's *nom de plume,* although there are two graves in the tomb. Some think Kamali was Jamali's wife, a sister, a poet, or a disciple.

The Jamali–Kamali Mosque and Tomb sit on top of a hill in the Mehaurli–Gurgaon Park, which contains a number of monuments in various stages of disrepair or restoration. The Tomb is a small beautiful ornate structure. Two of Jamali's verses adorn the ceiling. Side by side, inches apart, are two white marble graves, one Jamali's, the other, said to be Kamali's.

Karen Chase

Two Ghazals and One Fragment by Jamali

From the ceiling of the tomb

"Agar be kofr keshad sar siyah-kari-ye ma,
bovad be 'afw-e to cheshm-e omidvari-ye ma"

Even if our impious dark deeds amount to arrogant denial, yet still our hopeful eyes look to your forgiveness.

Here at your threshold we are ashamed even in front of the dogs, who get no rest at night because of all our weeping and lamenting.

If we gain the honour of being admitted behind the veil of your mystery, even the angels will be proud to serve us as guardians of the veil.

Men look on us with scorn, covered as we are with the dust of your roadway: but our very abasement is, in the eyes of those who know how to see, a cause of proud rejoicing.

Your clouds rain grace to wash away our dust, yet still the heart feels scalding wounds of shame.

When you are away, we are left alone and friendless: only the yearning for you keeps company in our grief.

Jamali, bring your woes to the threshold of the Friend, for there lies our salvation!

***"Ze hadd gozasht be 'eshq-e to bi-qarari-ye ma,
omid hast ke rahm avari be zari-ye ma"***

My restlessness, for love of you, has passed all bounds; yet still I hope you will have pity on my lack of calm!

Your mercy's beauty would never have appeared from behind the bridal veil, had not our sinfulness dared show its face.

Though we deserve your wrath for our sins, yet our eyes still look in hope to your grace.

We will reach the high honour of the spheres of compulsion and the angels, if once you deign to look on our lowly dust.

If we keep watch at the veil of your mysteries, angels will not be worthy to be our keepers.

One drop from the clouds of your generosity will wash away the dust of sin from the face of our shame.

From the fount of giving, throw a glance at Jamali, do not look only on our weakness and unripe works.

"Ay rahm-e to az ghazab bord gero,
way qahr-e to-ra lotf-e to farmud buro!"

Your mercy takes the prize from your wrath, your grace commands your wrath to go!

When we speak of the haystack of your mercy, our sins count not even as a grain.

Translated from Persian by Bruce Wannell